HERCULES

The Washington Monument

by Susan Ashley

Reading consultant: Susan Nations, M.Ed., author/literacy coach/consultant

WEEKLY WR READER®
EARLY LEARNING LIBRARY

Please visit our web site at: www.earlyliteracy.cc
For a free color catalog describing Weekly Reader® Early Learning Library's
list of high-quality books, call 1-877-445-5824 (USA) or 1-800-387-3178 (Canada).
Weekly Reader® Early Learning Library's fax: (414) 336-0164.

Library of Congress Cataloging-in-Publication Data

Ashley, Susan.
    The Washington Monument / by Susan Ashley.
      p. cm. — (Places in American history)
    Includes bibliographical references and index.
    Contents: Honoring the first president — Planning and building — The national mall —
Visiting the monument.
    ISBN 0-8368-4144-1 (lib. bdg.)
    ISBN 0-8368-4151-4 (softcover)
    1. Washington Monument (Washington, D.C.)—Juvenile literature. 2. Washington (D.C.)—
Buildings, structures, etc.—Juvenile literature. 3. Washington, George, 1732-1799—Monuments—
Washington (D.C.)—Juvenile literature. [1. Washington Monument (Washington, D.C.).
2. National monuments.] I. Title. II. Series.
F203.4.W3A845   2004
975.3—dc22   2003062108

This edition first published in 2004 by
Weekly Reader® Early Learning Library
330 West Olive Street, Suite 100
Milwaukee, WI 53212 USA

Copyright © 2004 by Weekly Reader® Early Learning Library

Editor: JoAnn Early Macken
Art direction, cover and layout design: Tammy Gruenewald
Photo research: Diane Laska-Swanke

Photo credits: Cover, title, pp. 10, 20, 21 © Gibson Stock Photography; p. 4 © Terry Ashe/Time Life
Pictures/Getty Images; p. 5, 16-17 Kami Koenig/© Weekly Reader Early Learning Library, 2004;
pp. 6, 11 © Stock Montage, Inc.; pp. 7, 12, 13, 15 © North Wind Picture Archives; pp. 8, 9, 18 © Hulton
Archive/Getty Images; p. 14 © N. Carter/North Wind Picture Archives; p. 19 © Mark Wilson/Getty Images

Printed in the United States of America

1 2 3 4 5 6 7 8 9 08 07 06 05 04

Table of Contents

The Washington Monument rises
above Washington, D.C.

Honoring the First President

The Washington Monument is the tallest building
in Washington, D.C. Its white marble tower rises
high above the city. It points straight up at the sky.

Washington, D.C., is the capital of the United States. The city was named for George Washington. The Washington Monument was built to honor him.

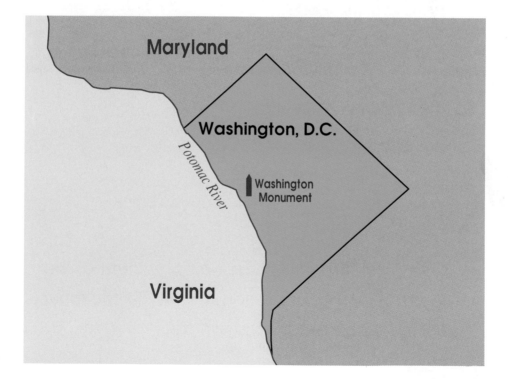

George Washington led American troops
during the Revolutionary War.

George Washington was the first president of the
United States. He was a hero of the Revolutionary
War. He helped Americans win their
independence.

After the war, Washington was elected to lead the new country. He served as U.S. president from 1789 until 1797. He died at his home in 1799. After his death, Americans wanted to build a monument to honor their first president.

George Washington was sworn in as the nation's first president in 1789.

Planning and Building

In 1833, people formed a group to build the monument. The group was called the Washington National Monument Society. They raised money to build the monument. They held a contest to find the best design. An architect named Robert Mills won the contest.

Robert Mills designed a tower with a circle of columns at the bottom.

Most monuments of the time were statues. Mills's design was different. It was an **obelisk** (AH-buh-lisk). An obelisk is a tall, narrow tower. The tower has four sides. It is wider at the bottom than it is at the top.

Columns circled the base of the design of the Washington Monument. Statues stood on top of the columns.

This obelisk was brought to England from Egypt in 1878.

Obelisks were popular in ancient Egypt. They were used to decorate temples. The Romans also built them. Ancient obelisks were always made of stone. The Washington Monument is also made of stone. It was built with blocks of marble.

The Washington Monument is made of marble.

Workers began building the monument in 1848. After six years, the Monument Society ran out of money. By that time, the monument was only 152 feet (46 meters) tall. That was 400 feet (122 m) shorter than it was supposed to be! It looked more like a tree stump than a monument.

The monument was not finished for many years.

The Civil War began in April 1861 at
Fort Sumter in South Carolina.

The monument stayed like that for many years.
In 1861, the Civil War began. There was no time
or money to work on the monument. After the
war, some people wanted to change the design.
Others decided to finish the job that was started.

Work did not start again until 1879. Thomas Casey came up with a simpler design. The new design had no columns or statues. It was a simple obelisk.

After the Civil War, Thomas Casey was in charge of finishing the monument.

© North Wind Picture Archives

© N. Carter/North Wind Picture Archives

Workers began adding new marble to the tower. The new marble was not the same color as the old marble. Today, it is possible to see where the old tower stopped and the new tower began.

The marble at the top of the tower is darker than the marble at the bottom.

People from all over the country donated stones. The stones line the inside of the monument. Each state sent a marble stone. Other countries also sent stones. The stones are carved with the names of the people and places they came from. In 1884, the monument was finished.

The monument was complete when the capstone, or top, was added.

© North Wind Picture Archives

The National Mall

The Washington Monument stands in the middle of the National Mall. The National Mall is a long park.

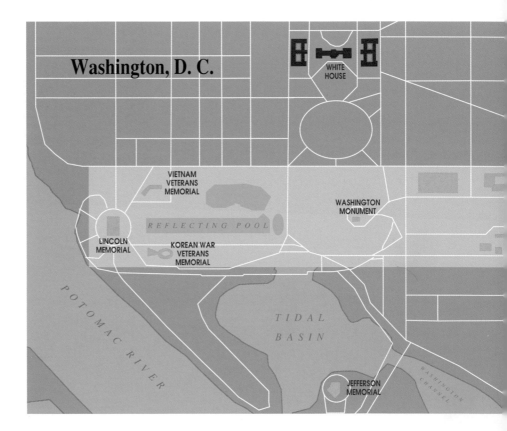

Washington, D. C.

WHITE HOUSE

VIETNAM VETERANS MEMORIAL

REFLECTING POOL

WASHINGTON MONUMENT

LINCOLN MEMORIAL

KOREAN WAR VETERANS MEMORIAL

P O T O M A C   R I V E R

T I D A L

B A S I N

WASHINGTON CHANNEL

JEFFERSON MEMORIAL

The Capitol building is at one end of the Mall.
It faces the Washington Monument.

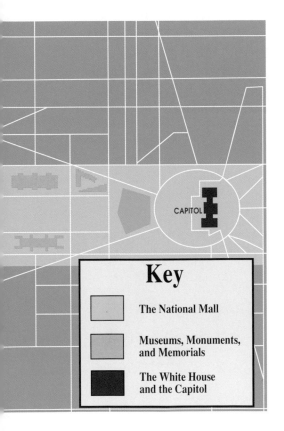

CAPITOL

Key

The National Mall

Museums, Monuments, and Memorials

The White House and the Capitol

The National Mall contains many monuments and museums.

In 1957, Martin Luther King, Jr., spoke about freedom on the National Mall.

The Lincoln Memorial is a monument to President Abraham Lincoln. It stands at the other end of the Mall. Museums and monuments line both sides of the Mall. They teach people about U.S. history.

Many important events take place near the Washington Monument. People stand in its shadow to hear famous speeches. The Mall is also the site of great concerts.

On the Fourth of July, fireworks burst over the Mall. Huge crowds gather around the Washington Monument. They celebrate the nation's birthday.

Fireworks light up the sky over the Washington Monument.

From the top of the monument, visitors can see the Capitol and many other sights.

Visiting the Monument

Many people visit the Washington Monument. A statue of George Washington stands in the lobby. Visitors can take an elevator to the top of the monument. From there, they can view the whole city.

The Washington Monument reminds people of the country's first president. George Washington believed in freedom. He believed in serving his country. These things are still important to Americans.

The Washington Monument honors George Washington and the country he served.

Glossary

ancient — very old

capital — the city where a country's government is located

honor — to show respect

independence — freedom

line — to be placed inside or along something

marble — a stone often used in building

monument — a building made to honor and remember an important person or event

pyramid — a shape with a square bottom, a pointed top, and four triangle sides

For More Information

Books

Dubois, Muriel L. *The Washington Monument.* Mankato, Minn.: Bridgestone Books, 2002.

Ford, Carin T. *George Washington: The First President.* Berkeley Heights, NJ: Enslow Publishers, 2003.

Schaefer, Lola. *The Washington Monument.* Chicago: Heinemann Library, 2002.

Web Sites

Memorial Stones
www.nps.gov/wamo/memstone.htm
View the stones donated by states and people from around the world

Washington, D.C. Sightseeing Map
sc94.ameslab.gov/TOUR/tour.html
Click on the Washington Monument for a photo and more information

Washington Monument web site
www.nps.gov/wamo/home.htm
More information about the monument and George Washington

Index

About the Author

Susan Ashley has written over eighteen books for children, including two picture books about dogs, *Puppy Love* and *When I'm Happy, I Smile*. She enjoys animals and writing about them. Susan lives in Wisconsin with her husband and two frisky felines.